Your Guide to Teaching
The Guitar

(And making a living doing what you LOVE)

by *Michael Grande*

I0428137

My name is **Michael Grande**, the creator of the **Card Chords**. I have been teaching people for over 30 years how **NOT to SUCK** at playing the Guitar!

I have made an excellent living teaching guitar and have used these very same methods in this book to grow my music lesson business into three music schools, employing over forty coaches.

I wrote this book for all of those guitar players who always had the desire to teach the guitar but was unsure where to start.

This book gives you a step by step guide on what you should be teaching beginner guitar players.

This book introduces the most common chords used. While I realize it is a 'cheap plug', I would be remiss to not mention the **Card Chords**. Card Chords act as a visual aid as well as a flash card that can be used while learning the beginner chords. Once in place, your student will be able to hear if the chords they are playing are correct while learning to play the chord.

Instead of teaching your students music theory, or learning to read music using a Mel Bay book, we start beginner guitar players off with the most common chords.

LOOK FOR THE QR CODES. This is an interactive handbook in that I provide short video lessons to help you explain some of the methods used to teach in this book.

TAKE IT SLOW! I have learned that the majority of people who want to learn to play guitar do not want to be rock stars. The moment I stopped teaching kids complicated guitar solos and started to teach them the songs and music they wanted to learn, my business took off.

Remember, it isn't about the music you want to teach, it's about teaching the music they want to learn.

I am starting off this handbook with goal setting. I have found that setting goals has made a significant impact on the learning process with my students. Be sure you set aside a few minutes to write out your students goals. Setting goals is not just for learning music, but it is also a life skill.

And most importantly...**HAVE FUN!**

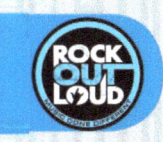

SETTING GOALS

To help you with your goals, we created Rock-N-Roll-O-Scope. Unlike a Horoscope that 'predicts' your future, we want YOU to predict yours. Spend a moment with your coach and write out your goals. They can include anything from learning how to play some chords, to learning how to play your favorite song. We are confident by the end of this book you will have achieved your goals!

Date: _____

Goal 1 _____

Goal 2 _____

Goal 3 _____

One Book in Two Parts

Part One introduces the most popular open chords along with songs you can play along to. We have also included QR codes that will direct you to a YouTube video that will help explain the songs in more detail. We've also included Bar and V-Form Chords as well.

Part Two introduces you to consecutive picking along with chromatic scale exercises to help build the strength in your left and right hands. The QR codes included in these lessons will direct you to a YouTube video that will help explain the lessons included in this book in more detail.

As you work though this book, you'll have a deep understanding of Major and minor chords and begin to develop the skills that will get you ready to start playing lead guitar, which will be the focus in our next book .

Now let's **ROCK OUT LOUD!**

Introducing the
CARD CHORDS

(Yes, this is a cheap plug, however, these interactive Card Chords
will help you learn to play guitar much quicker.)

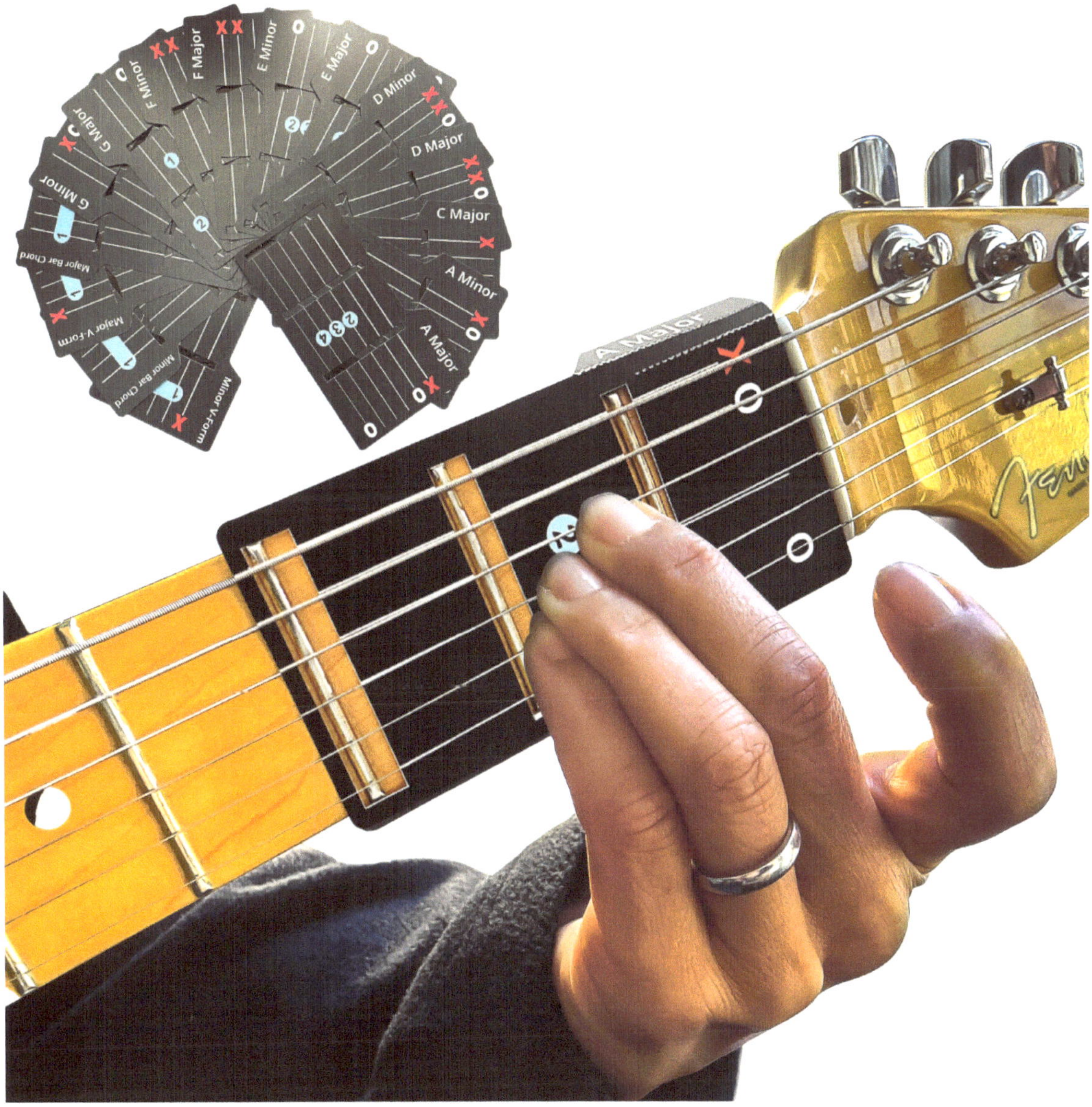

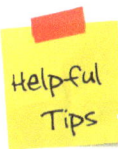

Helpful
Tips

To Purchase a FULL SET of Card Chords (there are **15** of the
most common chords included in the deck), **visit**
CardChords.com

Getting Started Withh
CARD CHORDS

Each Card Chord comes with a perforated tab. This tab can be bent to keep the Card Chord in place when positioned between the strings and the fretboard.

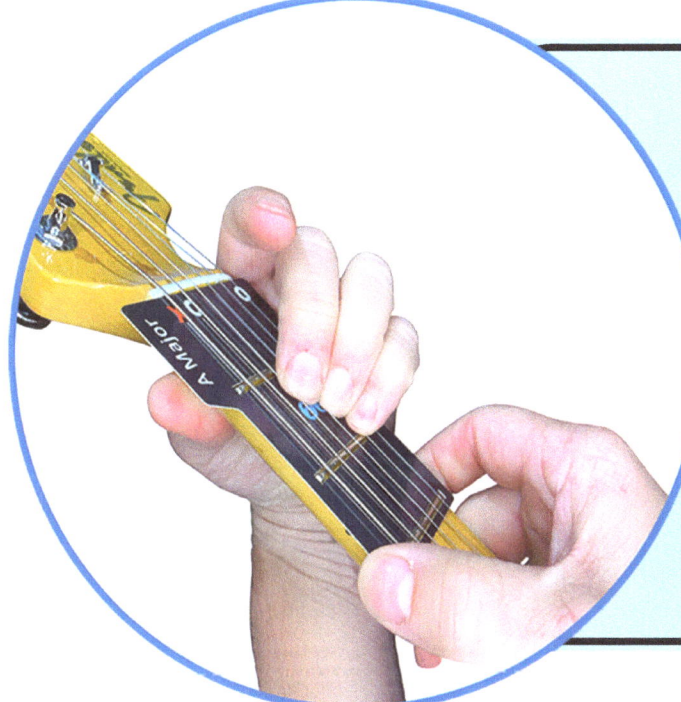

Place the Card Chord between the Strings and the Fretboard. Slide the Card Chord up the neck until it hits the nut. The Fret Cutouts will lock the card in place.

With your **Right Hand**, position the Card Chord so the strings line up with the Card Chord.

While holding the Card Chord in place with your **Right Hand**, using your **Left Hand**, place your fingers on the notes indicated on the Card Chord.

Because all guitars are setup different, the height between the strings and the fretboard will vary from Guitar to Guitar.

To prevent the Card Chord from falling off the guitar while in place, we created perforations on the **TAB's** of the Card Chord.

These **TAB's** can be bent to fit snuggly along the neck of the guitar, preventing the Card Chord from falling off the neck when in position.

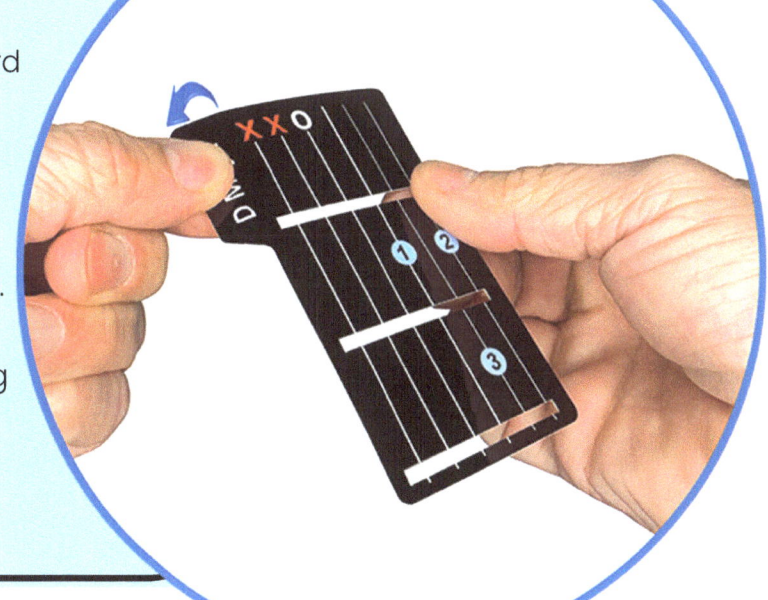

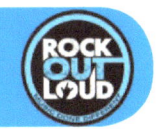

TABLE OF CONTENTS

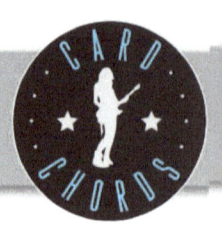

Placing your thumb in the back of the middle of the neck will allow you to play the notes on the tip of your fingers.

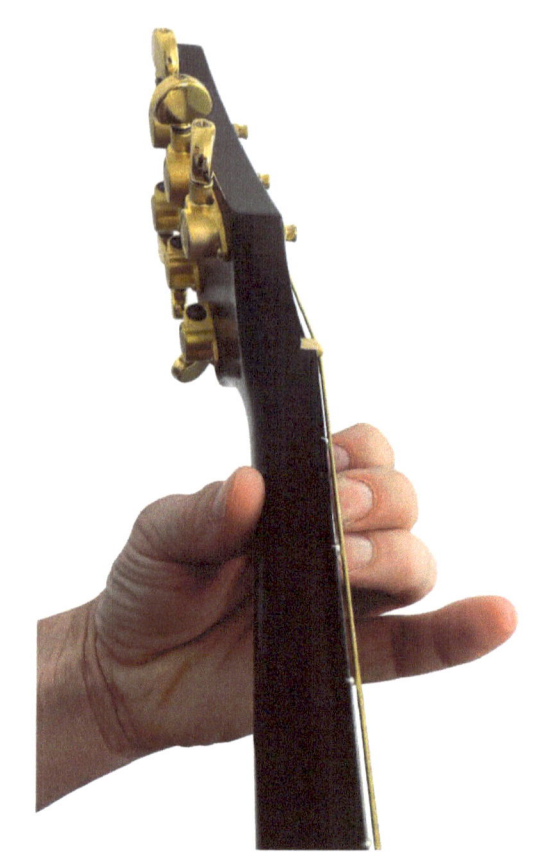

Notice the arch of the fingers. This will prevent your fingers from touching other strings when played

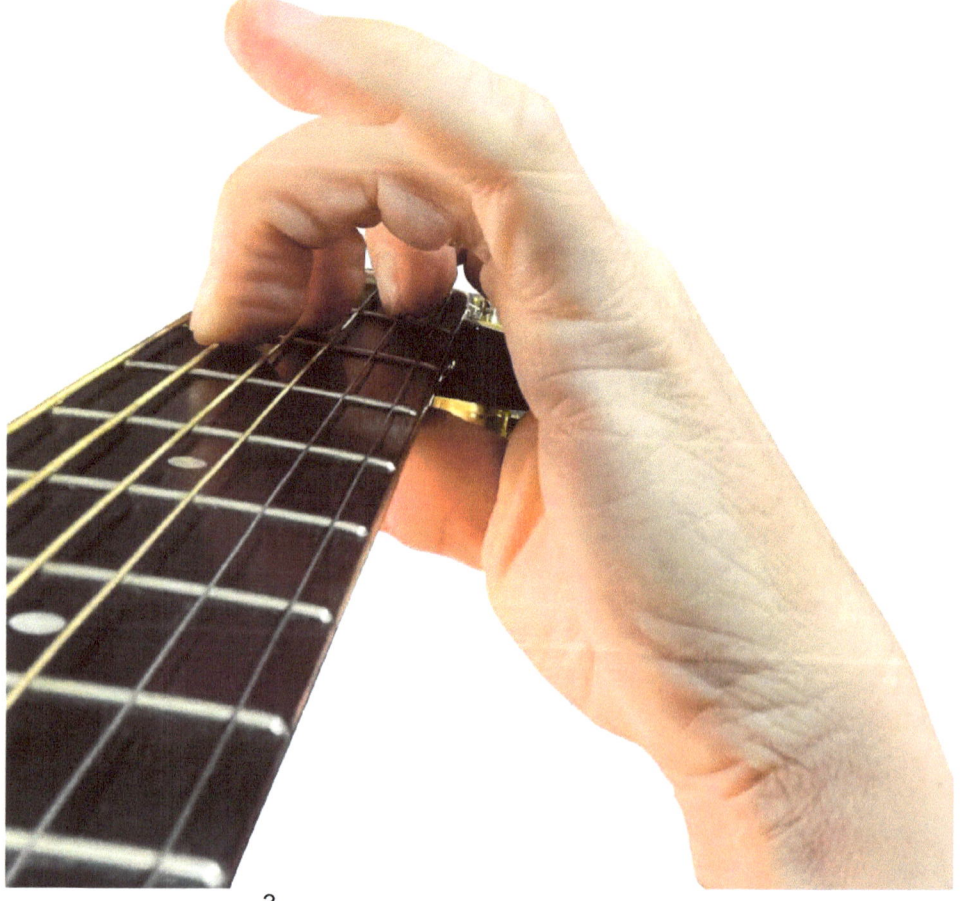

Scan to view the video tutorial

INTRODUCING the C Major Chord

The **C Major** chord is played using 3 fingers and 5 strings. Notice you have **X**'s and **O**'s. The **X** indicates that you do not play that string. **O**'s indicate that those open strings are played.

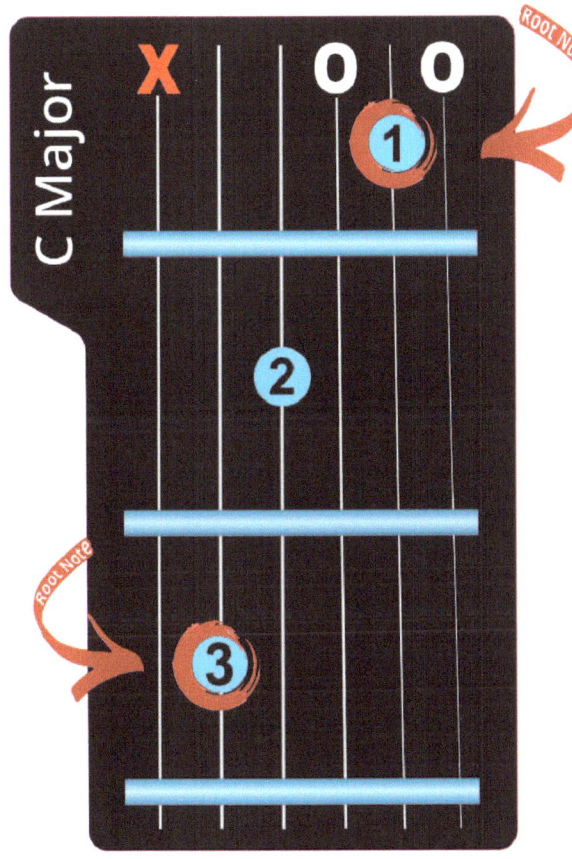

*What is a **Root** Note? And why you need to know where they are.*
Root Notes are used to identify the names and position of a Chord or Scale.

For example; a C Major chord has 3 notes; a C, E and G. **Root notes** are identified using a **RED** circle.

In order to find out where to play a C Major chord you need to find where the C notes are. In the example to the left, each C note in a C Major chord is circled in **RED**. If you placed those same circled notes on a D note, you would have a D Major chord.

*Chords and scales will often have 2 or 3 Root Notes. This means these notes repeat.

Starting on the 5th string, play each note, one at a time. If you do not hear the note come out, make sure you are using the tip of your finger to play the notes.

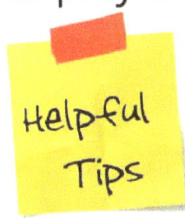

Be sure your thumb is properly placed on the back of the middle of the guitar neck. This will allow your fingers to be arched so you can use the tips of your fingers.

INTRODUCING the
D Major and D minor

As you can see, the fingering for these chords is different. However, we have one note in common between them (the **Root** note).

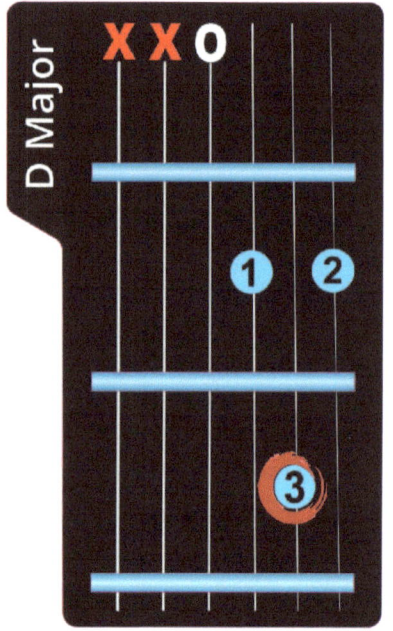

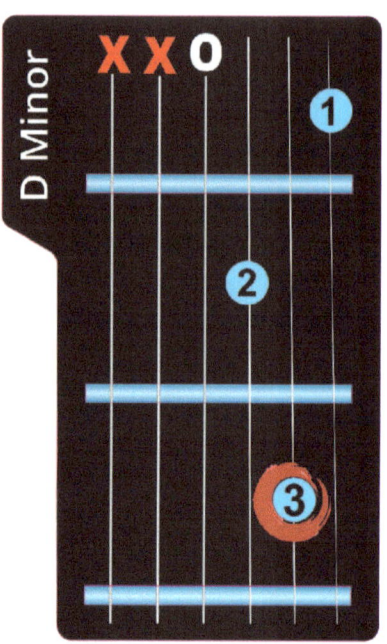

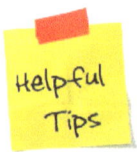

Keep your **3rd finger** on the second string when switching between the D Major and the D minor.

NOTES:

INTRODUCING the
G Major and G minor

The **G Major** chord uses 4 fingers, and all 6 strings are played. Notice the **G minor** chord only plays 4 strings. Your 5th string is muted using your 2nd finger and you don't play the 1st string.

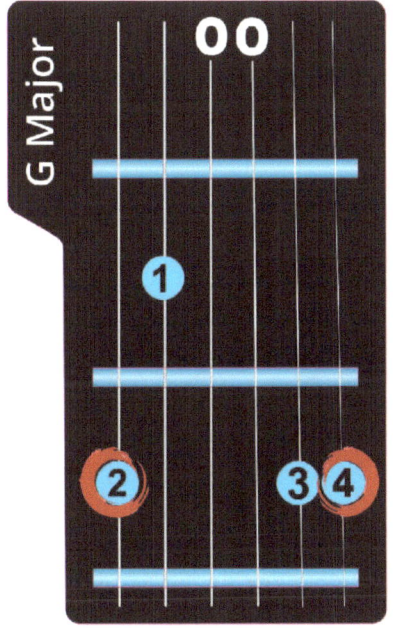

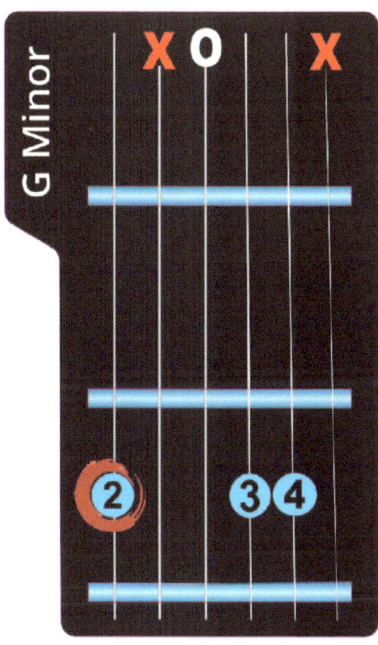

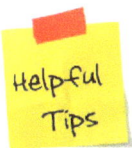

When transitioning between the G Major and G minor, keep your 2nd finger in place and bring up your 3rd and 4th fingers together. And don't forget to pick up your 1st finger.

NOTES:

6

KNOCKIN ON HEAVEN'S DOOR
by Bob Dylan

Verse 2X
Chorus 2X

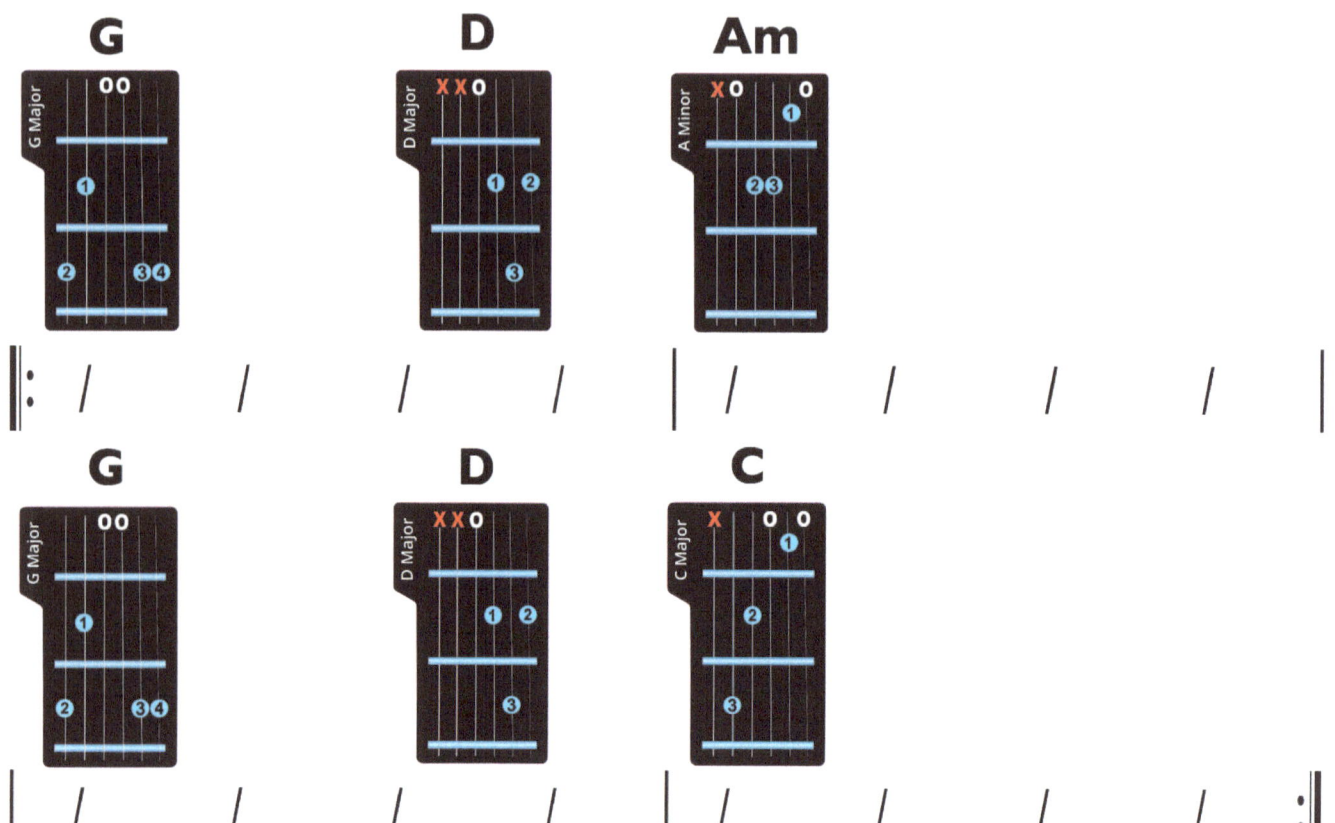

WATERMELON SUGAR
by Harry Styles

Verse 4X
Chorus 2X

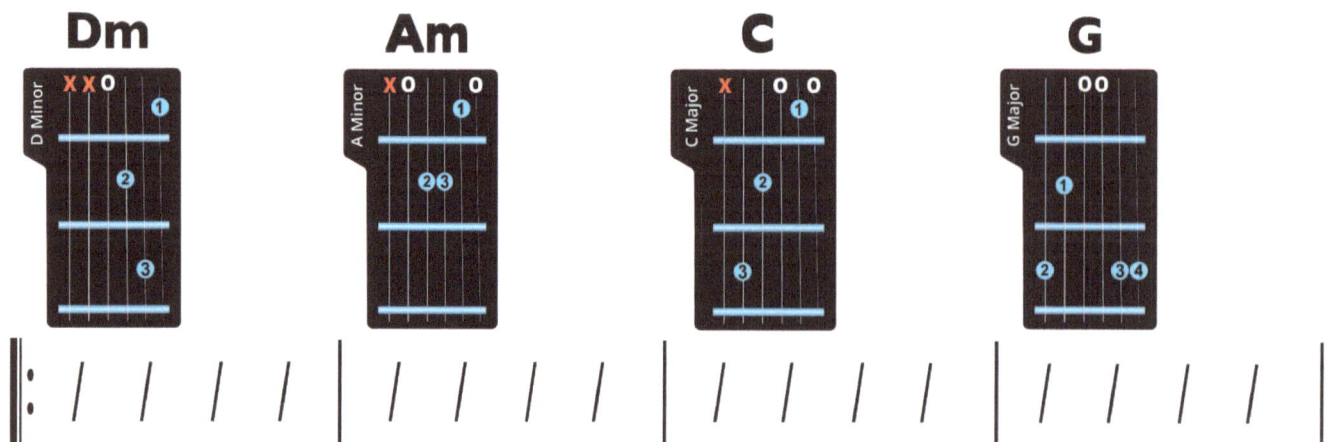

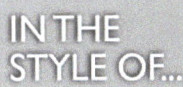
TWIST AND SHOUT
by The Beatles

Verse 4X
Chorus 4X

D   **G**   **A**

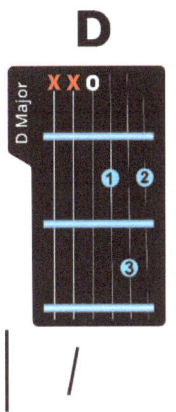 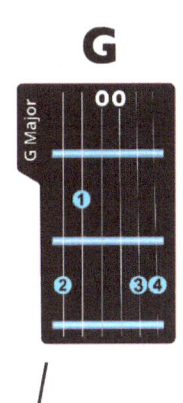 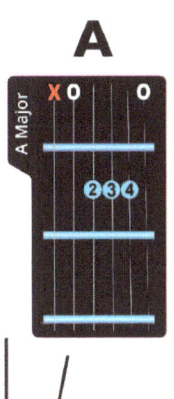

| | / | / | | / | / | | / | / | :||

A⁷   There is an Open G String added

* Note this is <u>NOT</u> an A Major Chord. It's an A Dominant 7

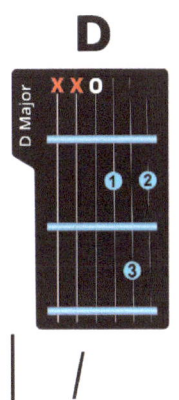

| / | / | | / | / | / | | / | / | / | | / | / | / | |

"Ahhh's" 4X

D   **G**   **A**   **G**

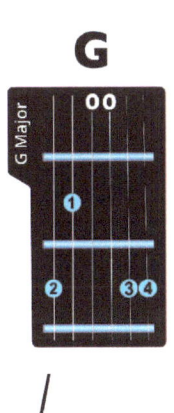 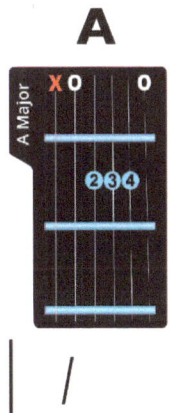 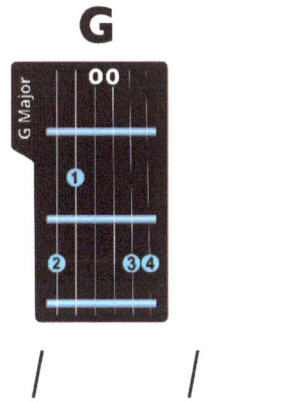

| / | / | | / | / | | / | / | | : ||

Guitar Solo 4x

BLUE SUEDE SHOES

by Elvis Presley

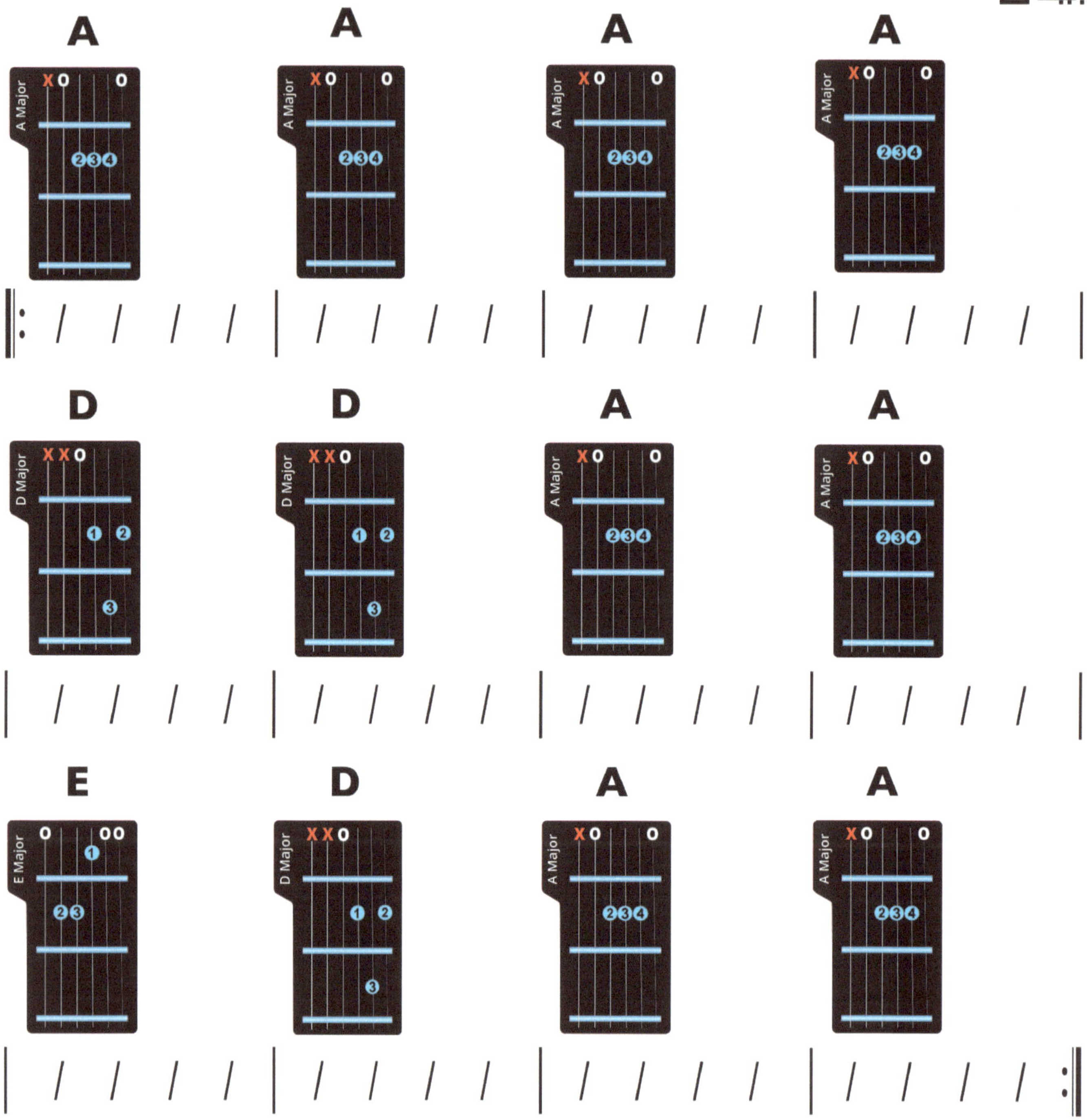

A   **A**   **A**   **A**

𝄆 / / / / | / / / / | / / / / | / / / / |

D   **D**   **A**   **A**

| / / / / | / / / / | / / / / | / / / / |

E   **D**   **A**   **A**

| / / / / | / / / / | / / / / | / / / / 𝄇

FUN FACT

Blue Suede Shoes is based around the 12 Bar Blues. The 12 Bar Blues is a common chord progression used to write many songs. We will be learning more about the 12 Bar Blues at a later time.

BROWN EYED GIRL
by Van Morrison

Verse 4X
Chorus 2X

G	C	G	D

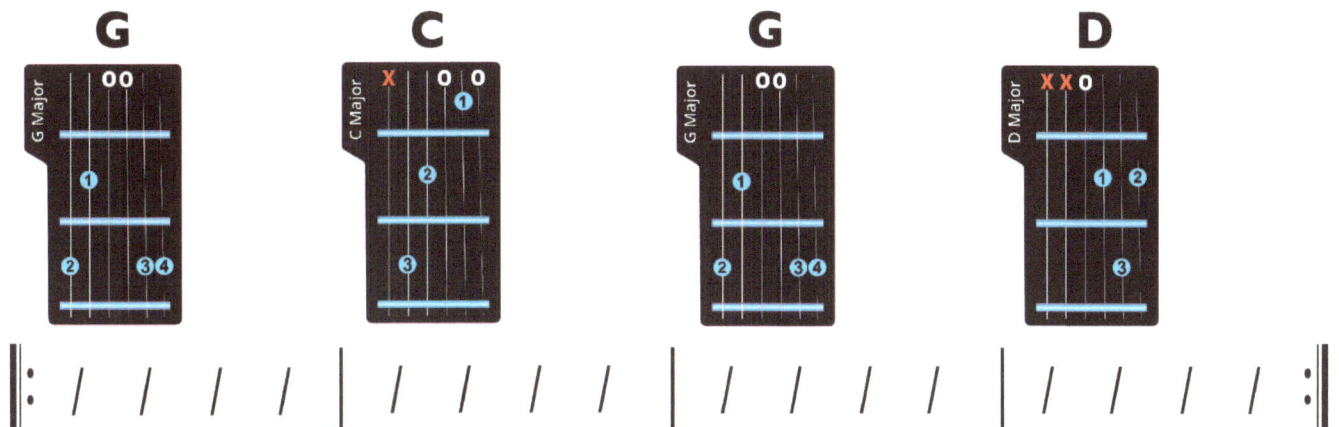

Pre-Chorus 1X

C	D	G	Em

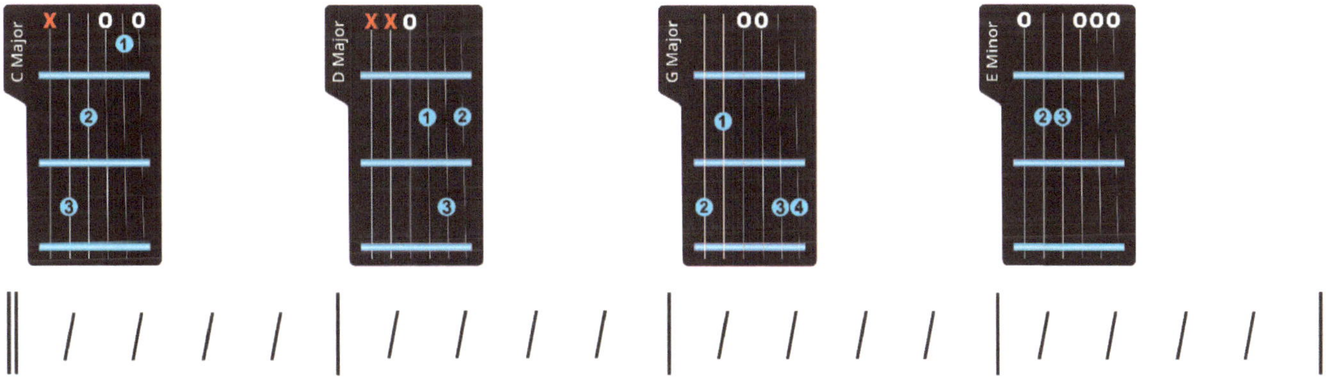

C	D	G	D

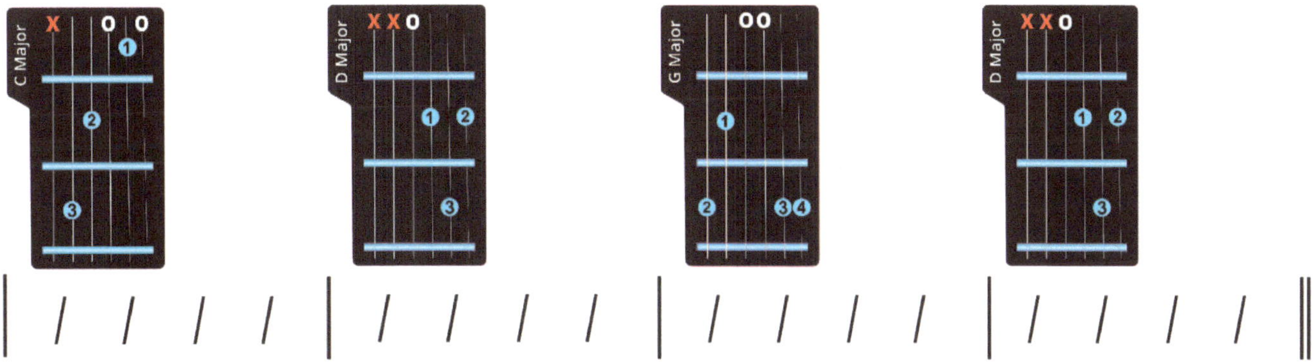

INTRODUCING the
F Major and F minor

The **F Major** chord shares some similarities to the C Major chord. It is important to note that your 1st finger is barring the 1st and 2nd string. Which means you are playing 2 notes with your 1st finger. Your **F minor** chord bars 3 strings and you remove your 2nd finger.

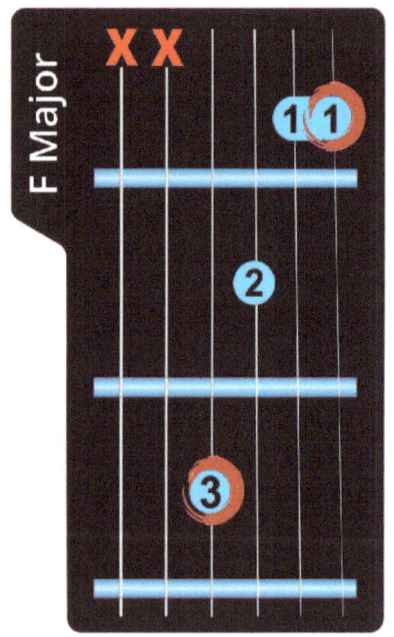

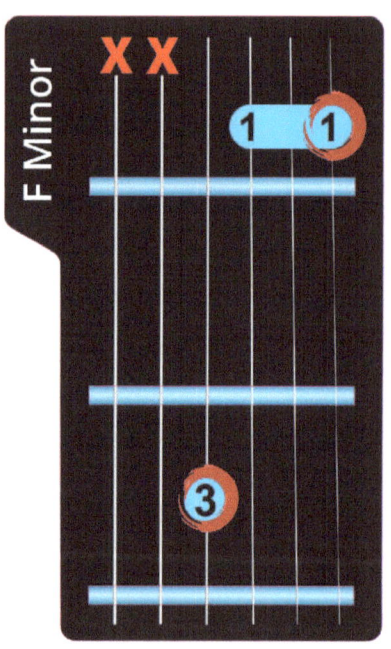

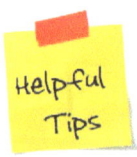 Keep your 3rd finger in place when switching between your F Major and F minor chord.

NOTES:

CIRCLES
by Post Malone

Verse 4X

C	G	F	Fm

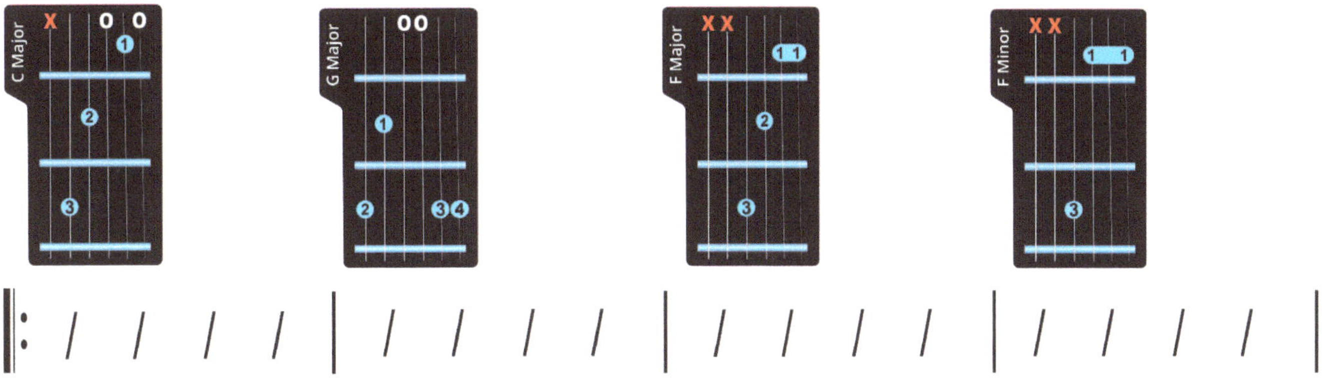

C   **G**   **F**   **G**

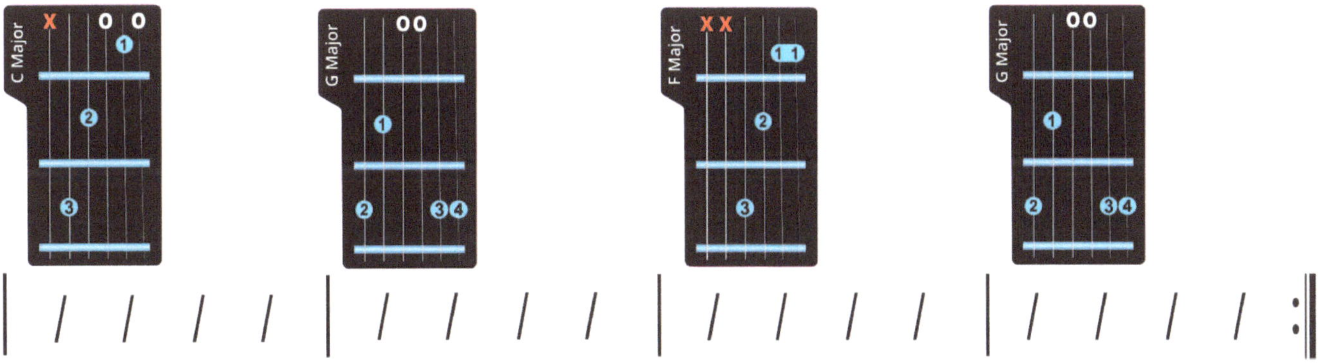

Chorus 4X

C	G	F	G

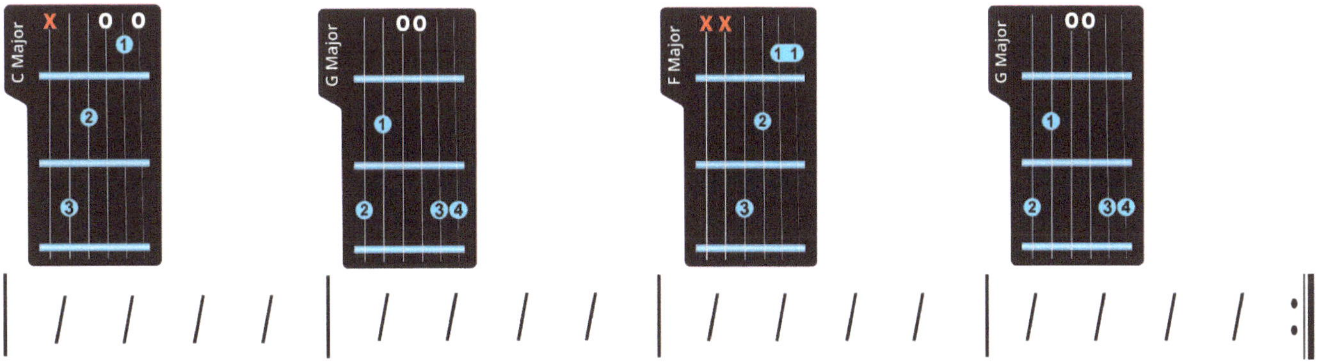

DID YOU KNOW?

Post Malone plays an F Major to an F minor chord for the Intro and Verses. This is considered a Key Change and is not often done in 'Pop' music.

LIVIN' ON A PRAYER
by Bon Jovi

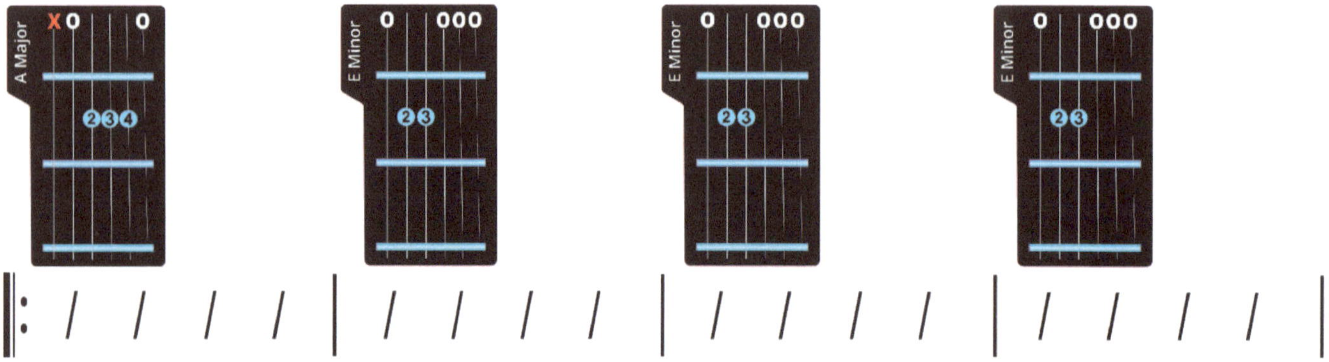

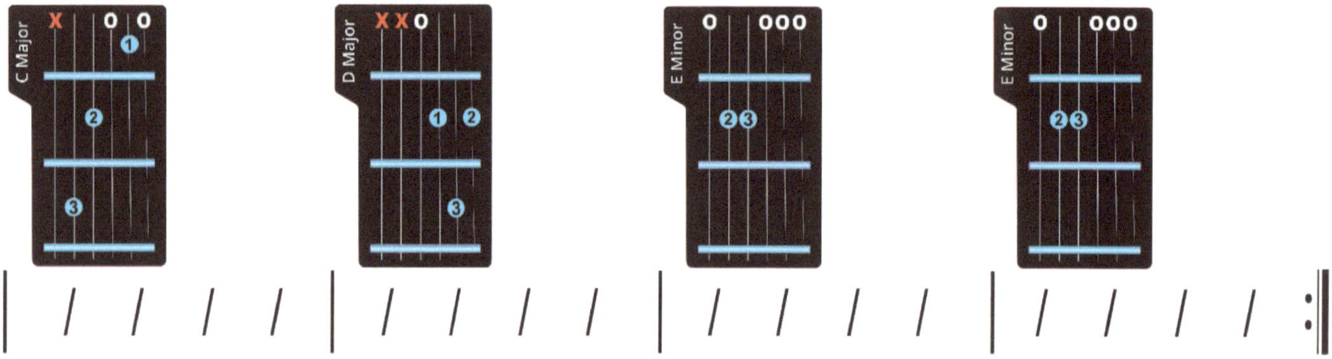

Verse 2X

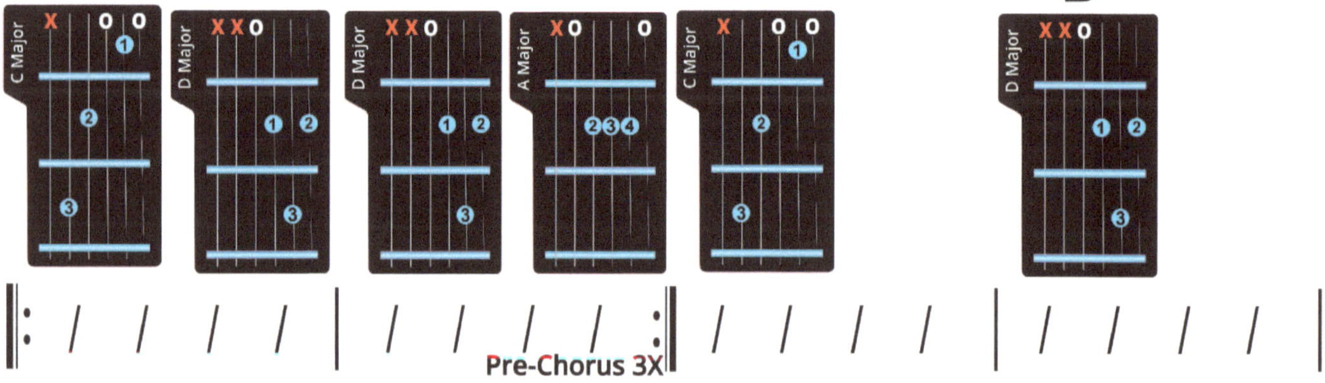

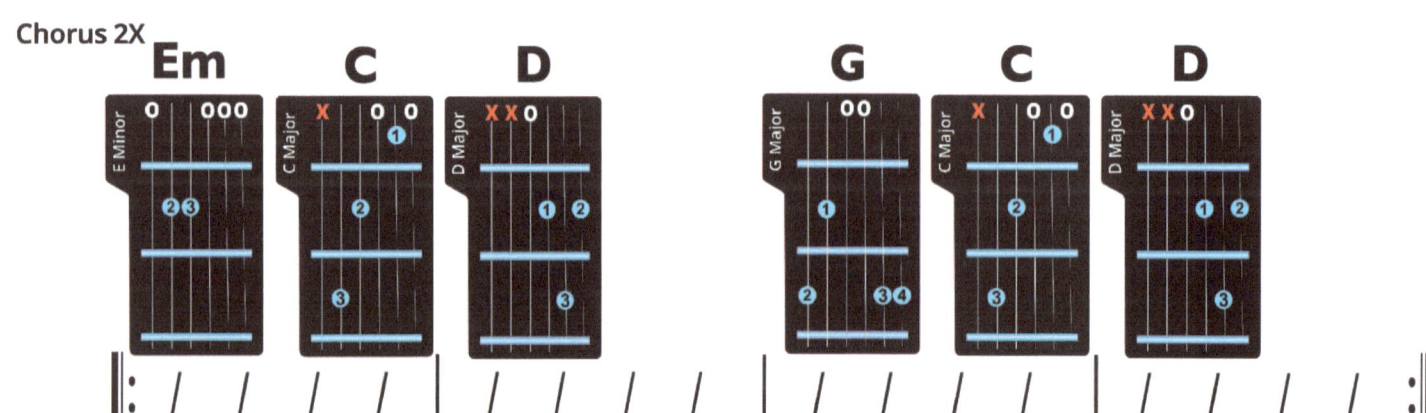

OPEN CHORDS

QUICK REFERNCE GUIDE

The key to playing open chords correctly starts with your **thumb**!* Yes your thumb. Placing your thumb on the back of the middle of the neck (on the hand playing the chords) will allow you to arch your fingers; allowing you to play the notes that are played before and after the note you are fingering.

Please refer to the video to better help you understand your proper thumb placement.

C
D Major — chord diagram (C Major): X 0 0, ① fret 1, ② fret 2, ③ fret 3

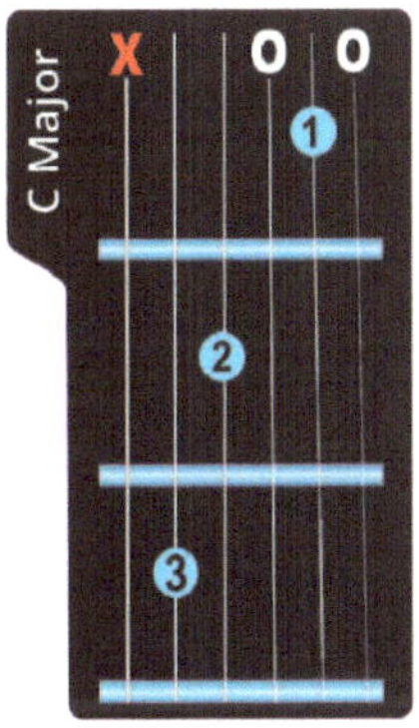

D
chord diagram (D Major): X X 0, ① ② fret 2, ③ fret 3

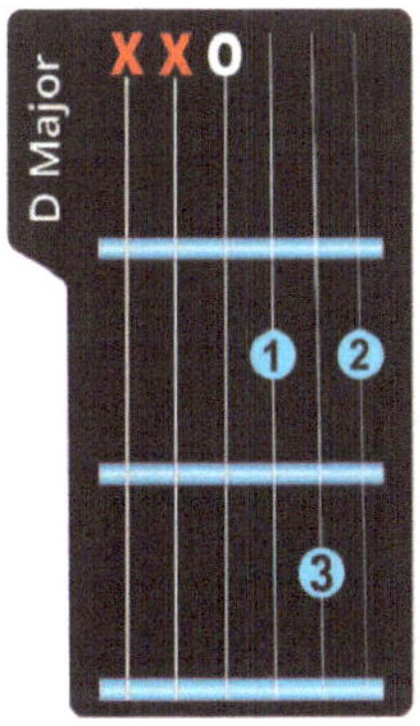

Dm
chord diagram (D Minor): X X 0, ① fret 1, ② fret 2, ③ fret 3

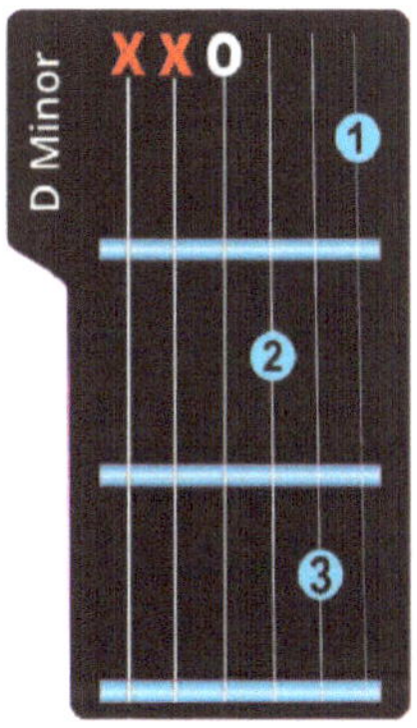

E
chord diagram (E Major): 0 0 0, ① fret 1, ② ③ fret 2

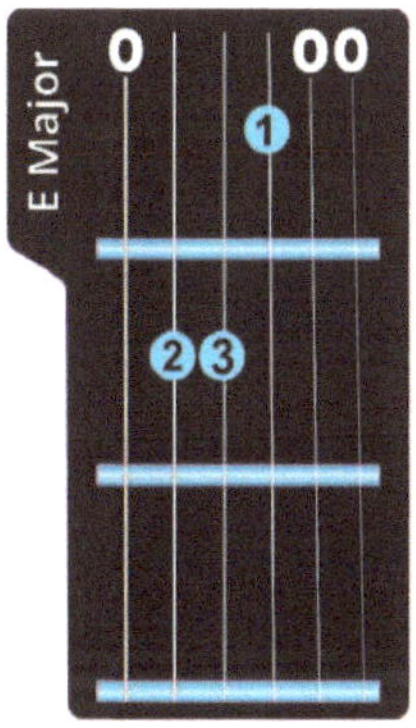

Em
chord diagram (E Minor): 0 0 0 0, ② ③ fret 2

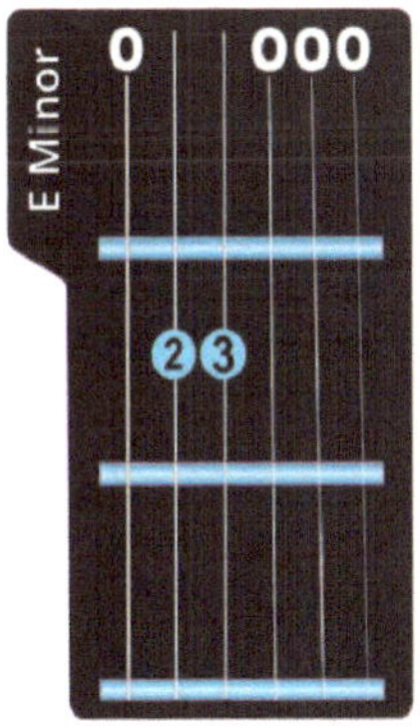

F
chord diagram (F Major): X X, ① ① fret 1, ② fret 2, ③ fret 3

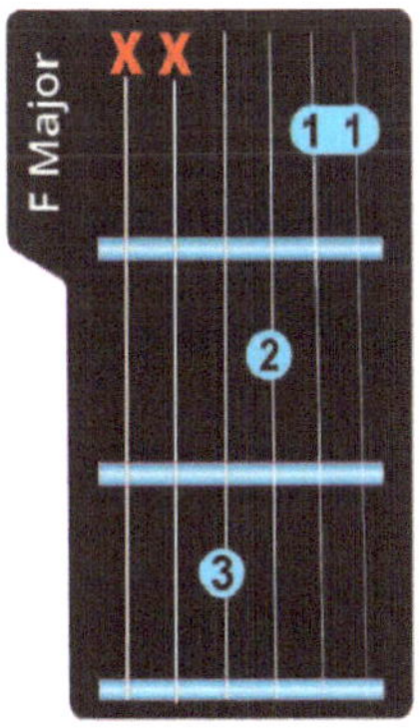

Fm
chord diagram (F Minor): X X, ① ① fret 1, ② ③ fret 3

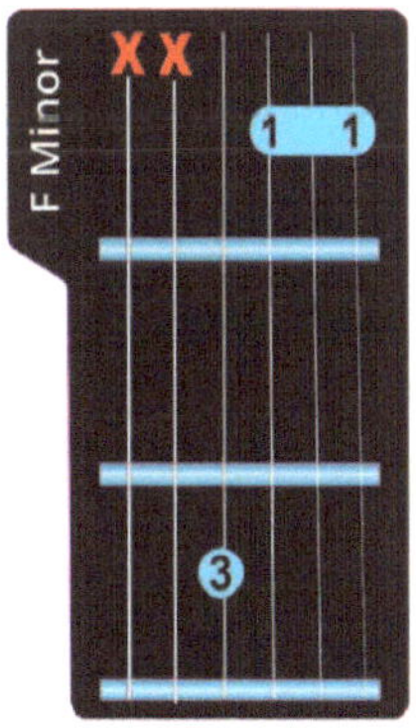

G
chord diagram (G Major): 0 0, ① fret 2, ② fret 2, ③ ④ fret 3

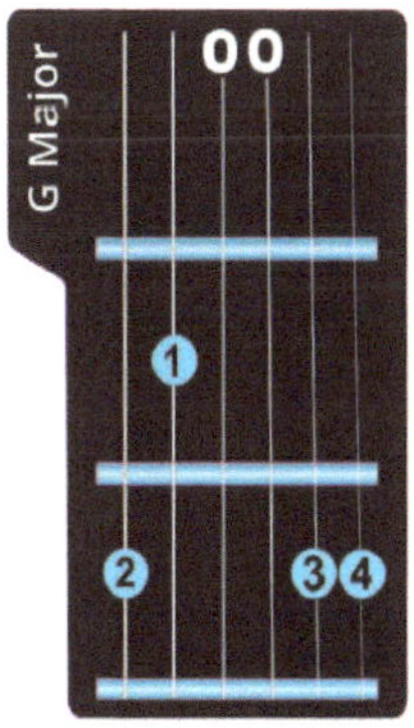

Gm
chord diagram (G Minor): X 0 X, ② ③ ④

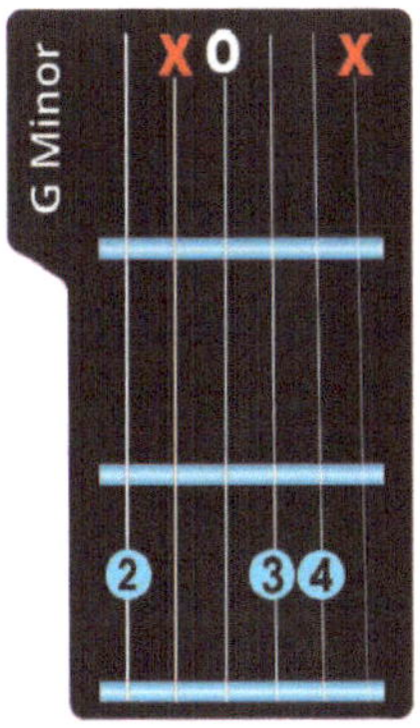

A
chord diagram (A Major): X 0 0, ② ③ ④ fret 2

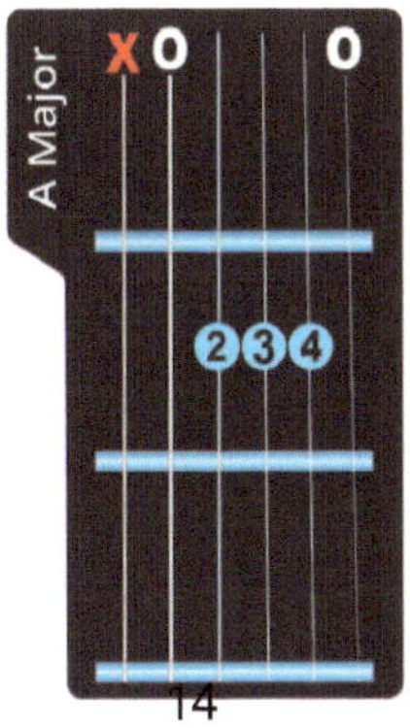

Am
chord diagram (A Minor): X 0 0, ① fret 1, ② ③ fret 2

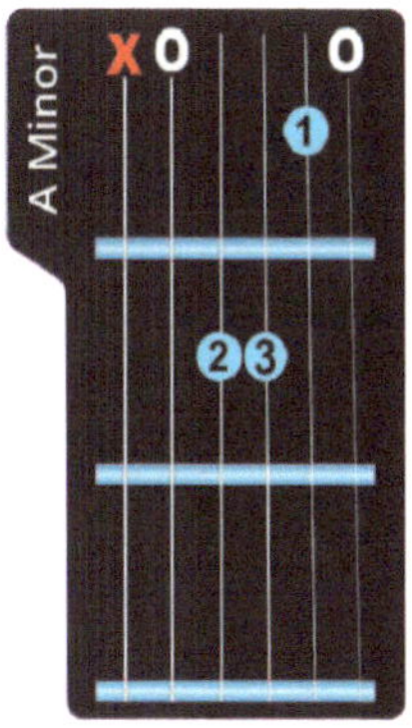

INTRODUCING
Major and minor Bar Chords
and why you NEED to know them!.

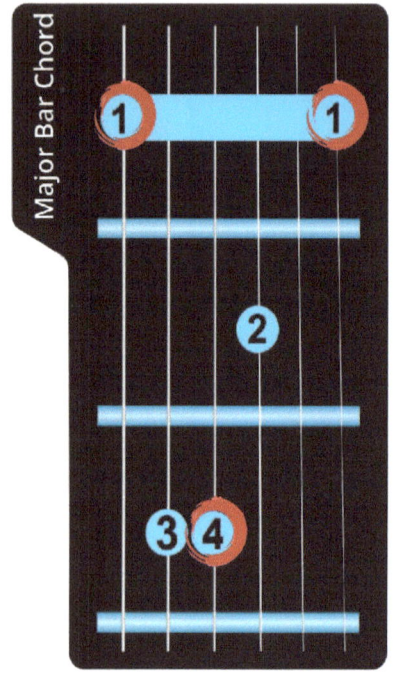

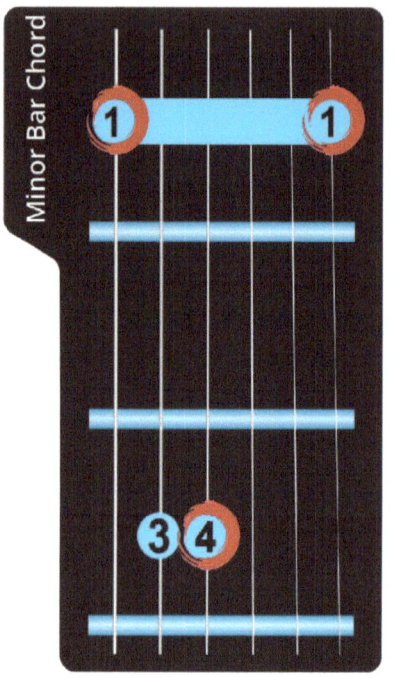

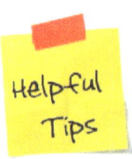 **Helpful Tips** Your 2nd finger is the only finger that makes the difference between a Major Chord and a minor Bar Chord.

COACH NOTES: *Explain how the Major and minor Chords can be played anywhere, allowing you to play Sharp (#) and Flat (♭) chords.*

INTRODUCING
Major and minor V-Form Chords
and why you NEED to know them!.

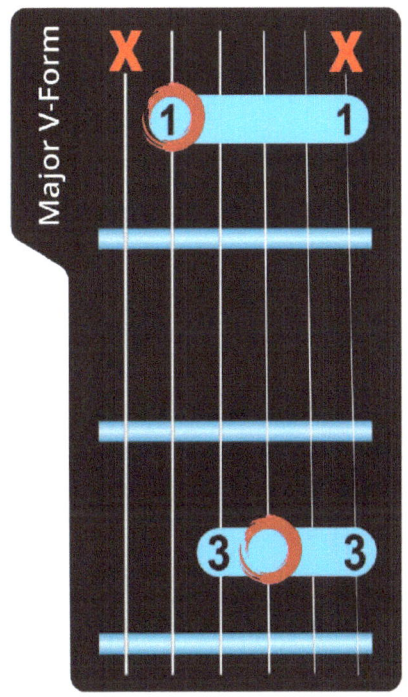

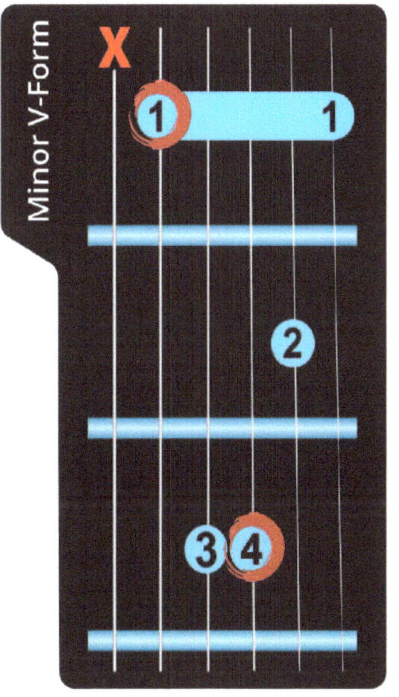

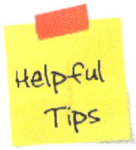
Your V-Form Major uses your 1st and 3rd fingers to bar the strings. Your V-Form minor looks identical to the Major Bar Chord.

COACH NOTES: *Explain how the Major and minor Chords can be played anywhere, allowing you to play Sharp (#) and Flat (♭) chords.*

CHROMATIC SCALES AND WARMING UP

Much like a runner who stretches their legs before they run; guitar players need to 'warm up' too. There is nothing better than Chromatic Scales when it comes to warming up your fingers.

Chromatic Scales can be played anywhere on the neck. There is no need to worry about the key you're in or where the root note is located. Simply place your hand on the fretboard and using one finger at a time, play 4 notes per string.

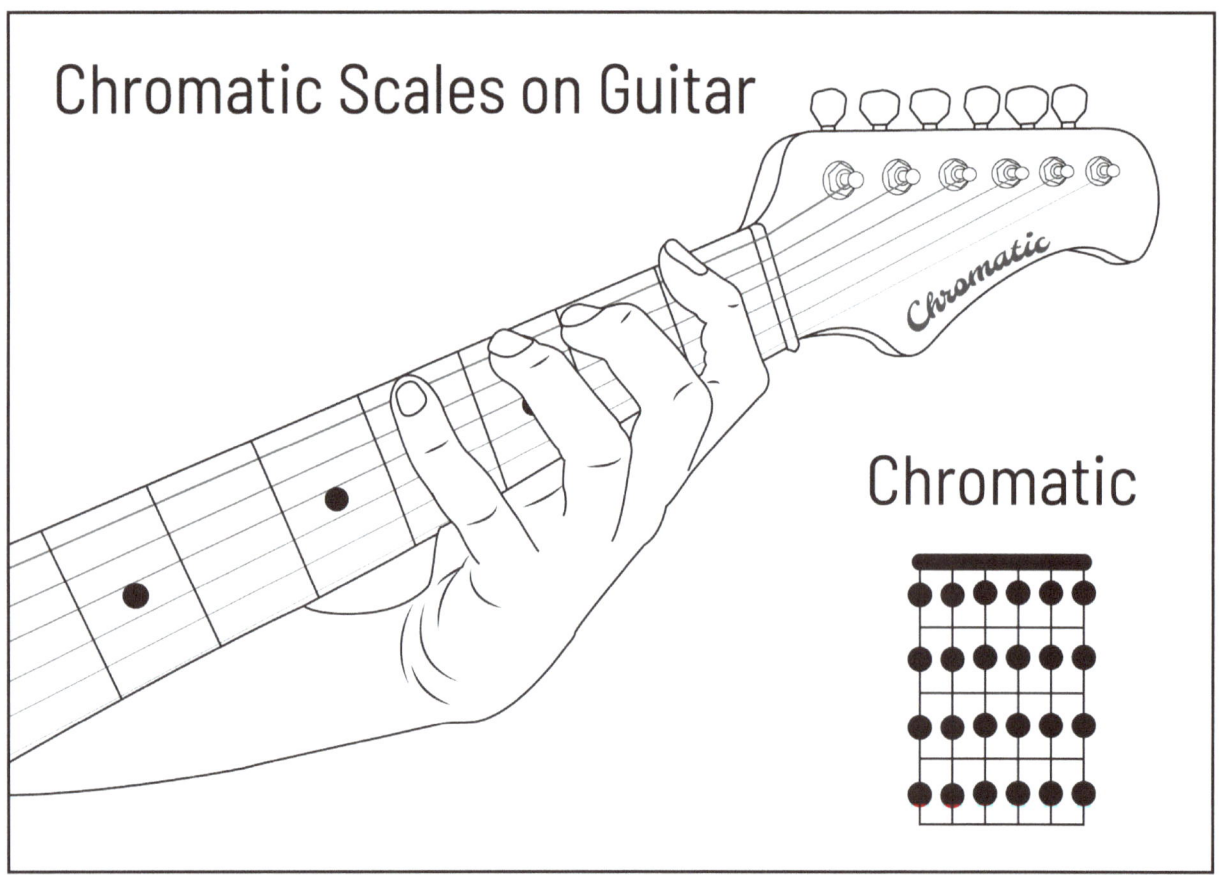

NOTES:

PICKING

Before we work on Chromatic Scale Exercises, it is important we know how to properly pick.

Consecutive (or) Alternative Picking is used when you are playing more than 1 note on the same string. The example below shows the pick hitting the string in a downwards motion, then upwards to hit the next note on the same string. This technique will help you develop your speed as you get more comfortable playing the guitar.

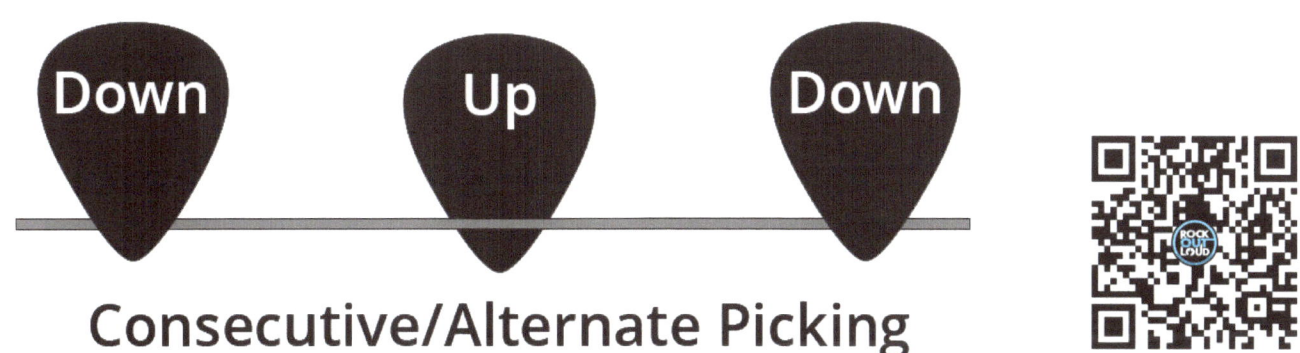

Consecutive/Alternate Picking

WARMUP EXERCISES using Consecutive Picking

While playing the 6th String (Low E String) to the 1st String (High E String) you pick DOWN then UP. Try this 1st exercise picking Down then Up from the 6th String to the 1st String.

This is an **ASCENDING** Pattern, which means you play this from the 6th String to the 1st String.

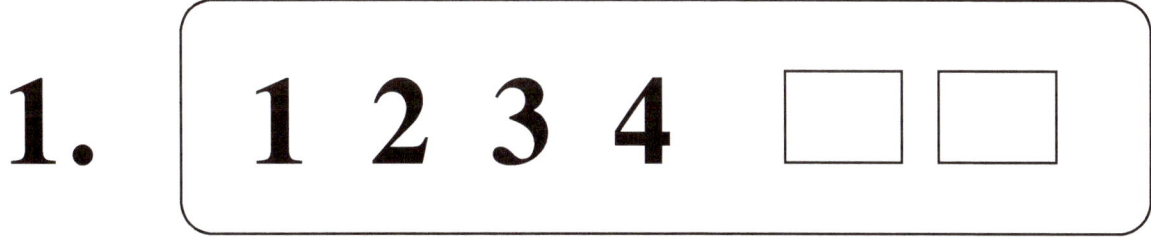

While playing the 1st String (High E String) to the 6th String (Low E String) you pick UP then DOWN. Try this 1st exercise picking Up then Down from the 1st String to the 6th String.

This is a **DESCENDING** Pattern, which means you play this from the 1st String to the 6th String.

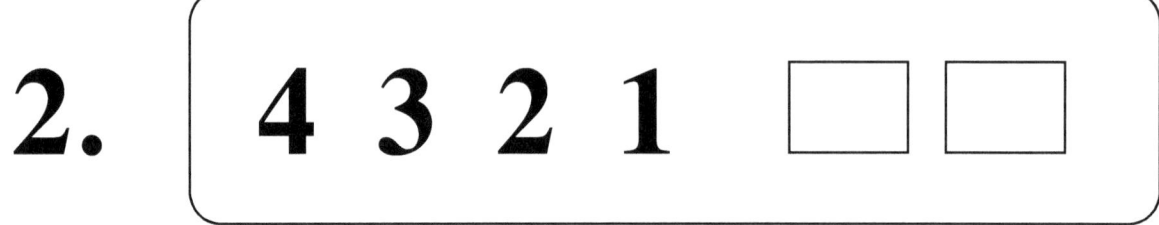

2. **4 3 2 1** ☐ ☐

While playing the 6th String (Low E String) to the 1st String (High E String) you pick DOWN then UP. Try this 1st exercise picking Down then Up from the 6th String to the 1st String.

This is an **ASCENDING** Pattern, which means you play this from the 6th String to the 1st String.

This next exercise is a little more challenging.
Notice how you play your 1st finger, then 4th finger, then 2nd finger, then 3rd finger.

3. **1 4 2 3** ☐ ☐

While playing the 1st String (High E String) to the 6th String (Low E String) you pick UP the DOWN. Try this 1st exercise picking Up then Down from the 1st String to the 6th String.

This is a DESCENDING Pattern, which means you play this from the 1st String to the 6th String.

This next exercise is a little more challenging.
Notice how you play your 4th finger, then 1st finger, then 3rd finger, then 2nd finger.

4. **4 1 3 2** ☐ ☐

THE METRONOME

Metronomes are used to help keep time. No matter what instrument you play, you should always learn to play with a metronome. As a teacher, I always had my students warm up to a metronome. Timing is measured in Beats Per Minute (BPM). A metronome that is set to 60 BPM means that there are 60 'ticks' per minute (or one 'tick' per second).

Another reason why I love to use the metronome is that it measures your progress. Very often you or your student may feel they have not gotten better at playing Guitar. This is when I put the metronome on and ask them to play at a higher BPM (for example; 68 BPM). Just being able to play at a higher speed is an indication you (or your student) has improved.

Note Values and how to count using a Metronome

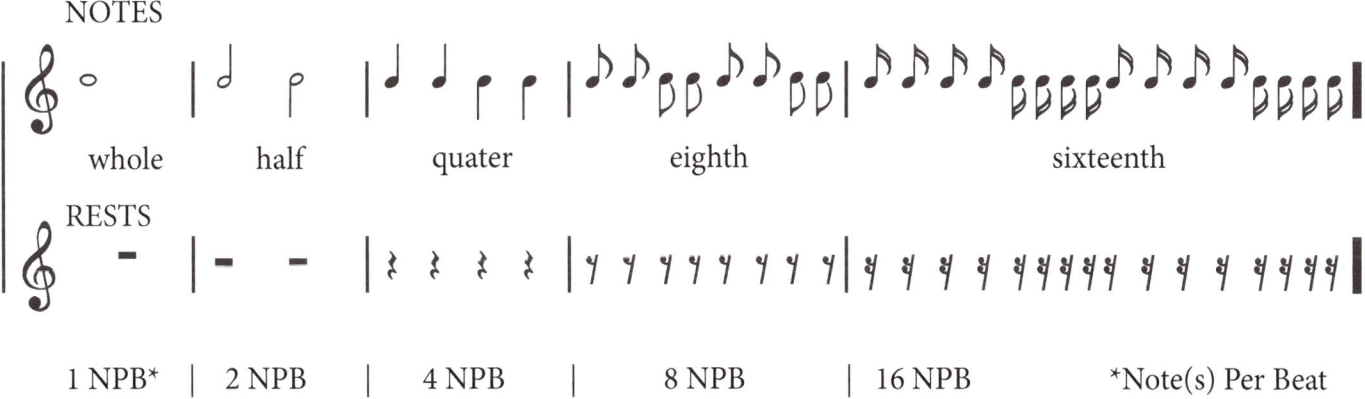

NOTES

whole   half   quater   eighth   sixteenth

RESTS

1 NPB* | 2 NPB | 4 NPB | 8 NPB | 16 NPB   *Note(s) Per Beat

Let's get started

If you don't own a metronome you can download a FREE metronome to your phone. Check the Apps Store or Google Play for free downloads. Alternatively, you can visit Metronomeonline.com and use the FREE metronome available online.

Set your metronome to 60. Using your chromatic scale, starting on any fret you feel comfortable (I.E. your 5th fret), play half notes. Half Notes are 2 notes per beat or 'tick'.

Be sure you consecutive pick. When you are comfortable playing from the 6th string to the 1st string and back, try to play Quarter Notes (4 notes per beat or 'tick'). As you get more and more comfortable, increase the amount of notes you play per beat.

NEVER increase the tempo on the Metronome until you can play Sixteen (16) notes per beat or 'tick'.

Are you up for a challenge?

Let's revisit the Chromatic Scale. Using the metronome on 60, playing quarter notes (4 notes per beat), try playing this pattern. From your 6th string to the 1st string, play 1st Finger, 4th Finger, 2nd Finger, 3rd Finger. Then, from the 1st string to the 6th string, play 4th Finger 1st Finger 3rd Finger 2nd Finger.

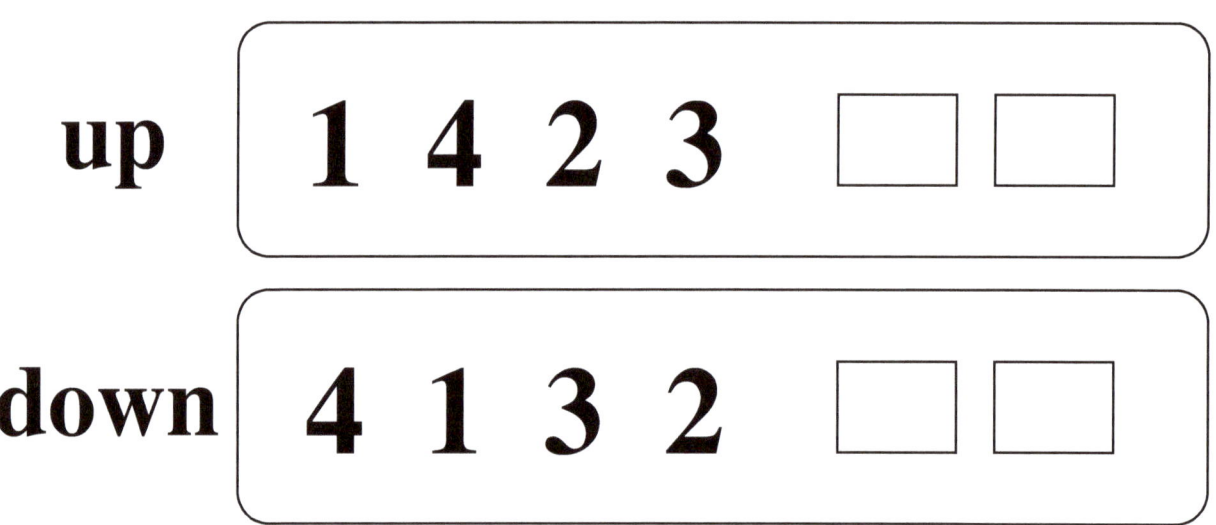

NOTES:

Knowing How To Find the Notes on the Neck

Knowing every note on the guitar is one of the most important parts of understanding the guitar! Unlike the piano, which has black keys and white keys to help identify the notes, the guitar does not have many 'visual aids' like the piano.

With just **ONE EXCEPTION. The Dots!** Most guitars have dots on the Fretboard. They are usually on the 3rd fret, 5th fret, 7th fret, 9th fret, 12th fret, 15th fret, 17th fret, 19th fret, etc. It is important to point out the 12th fret, which has (2) Dots.

The (2) Dots [12th fret] indicates where the open strings repeat. For example, if you play the Open E String, placing your finger on the E string at the 12th fret will give you the same note (an OCTAVE higher).

[Coach Notes: Fill out the notes on the neck with your student]

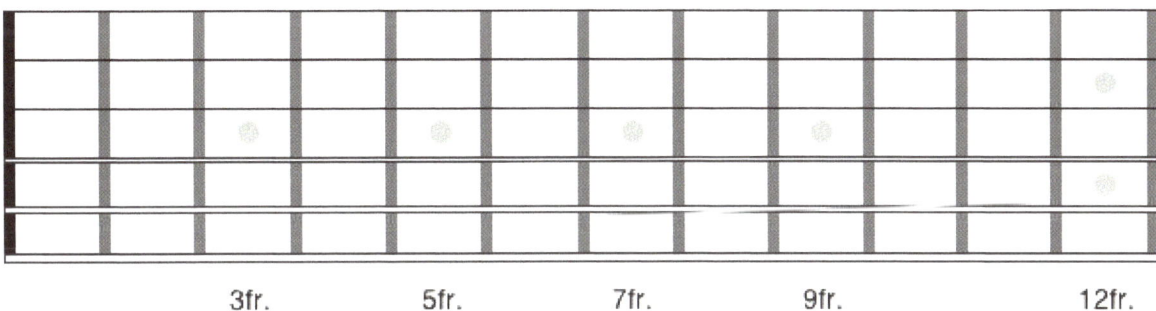

Use the example of the open G string to find out what note is on the 12th Fret, G string?

What is the name of the note that is played on the12th FRET, G Sting?
(Circle the correct answer)

| A | G | E | C |

Print out blank copies of the Guitar Neck to hand out to your students. Be sure they 'visualize' the notes as they repeat on the 12th Fret.

Point out that the 12th Fret are the same notes as the Open Strings:
<u>OPEN STRINGS:</u> **E A D G B E**   <u>12th FRET:</u> **E A D G B E**

By showing the students that the notes repeat at the 12th Fret, explain the reason why it is so important to know.

For example: If I asked to find an F Note on the G String (3rd String), Instead of counting from the Open G, to A, to B, to C, to D, to E, to F; it is much easier to find the G note (on the 12th Fret) and count back 1 whole step to the F note. This reduces a significant amount of time, and more importantly, it is less likely the student will make a mistake. (Counting up 10 frets on the G string to get to an F note leaves more opportunities to make a mistake. Whereas counting back 2 Frets from the G note on the 12th fret leaves less chances to make a mistake.)

NOTES:

The Guitar Hero Challenge:

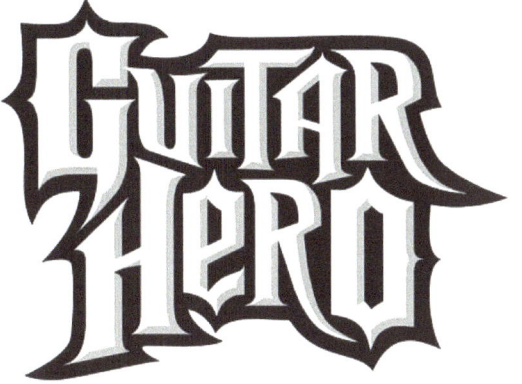

The **EASIEST-HARDEST** Exercise You'll Ever Do!

You will need a metronome for this exercise. Set the Metronome to 60 BPM. Pick any note (I.E. an F note). Each time you hear a beat on the metronome, play an F note. In many cases you will have 2 of the same notes on each string. For Example; an F note on the 1st Fret (Low E string), an F note on the 13th Fret (low E string), then the F note on the 5th String on the 8th Fret, then (if possible), the F Note on the 5th String on the 20th Fret, the an F Note on the 4th String on the 3rd Fret and so on.

Do this for every F note. Then pick another note and do the same thing.

Why is this so important?

Knowing the notes on the guitar will help you find the root notes to the scales you are playing.

NOTES:

Understanding MAJOR and MINOR Chords

Chords are made up of 2 or more notes played together. There are TWO types of Chords; the Major Chord and the minor Chord. The difference between a MAJOR CHORD and a MINOR CHORD is only **ONE** note; the **3rd**.

Major Triad has a (1) ROOT, (**Major 3rd**) and a (5th)

Minor Triad has a (1) ROOT, (**Flat 3rd**) and a (5th)

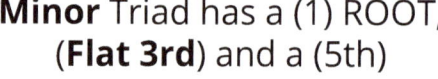

Major Chord Triad

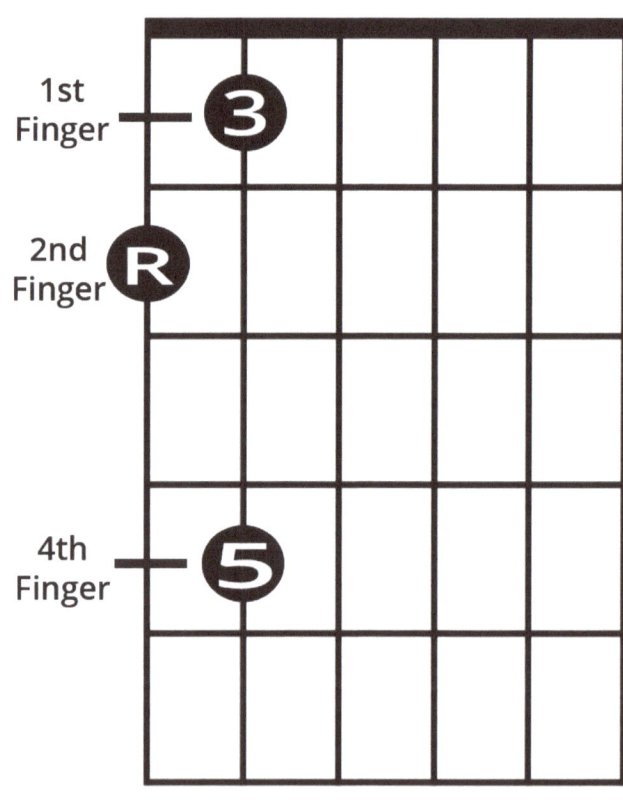

Minor Chord Triad

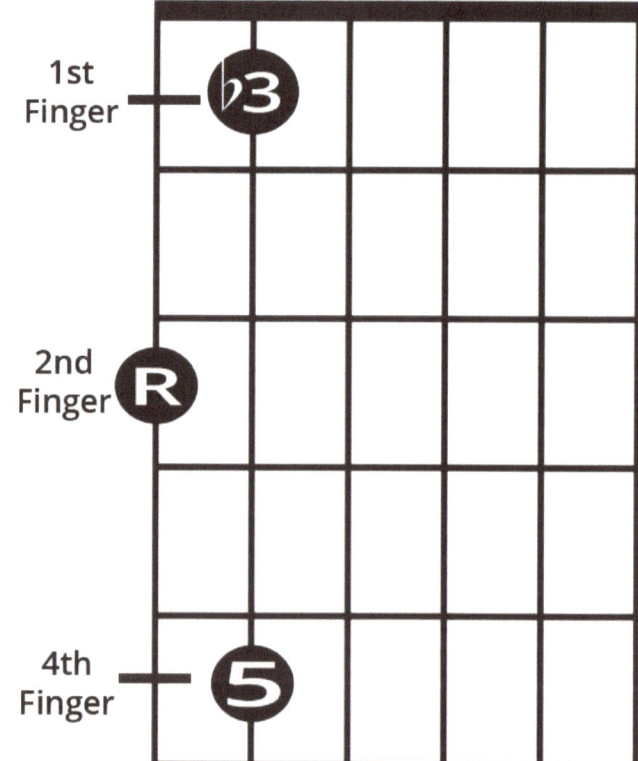

Now it's time to write out each note that makes up the chords below.

1. A Major □ □ □

2. E Minor □ □ □

3. B Minor □ □ □

4. C Minor □ □ □

5. E Major □ □ □

The Musicians Challenge: *Can you answer this?*

True or **False**:

The notes in an **A Major Chord** has an **A** note, a **Db** note and an **E** note.

True □   False □

26

A Coaches Teaching Moment

It is important to point out (based on the example of the (3) notes that appear in an A Major Chord are NOT an A, Db and an E. While a Db and a C# sound the same, you cannot call the note a Db.

Here's why...

A Triad consists of a ROOT (**1**) a (**3**) and a (**5**).

Now, take the Notes (Letters): **A**(1) a **C#** (3rd) and an **E** (5th). *If you add the Db instead of the C#, you are adding a 4th and not a 3rd.* You must <u>always</u> have a 3rd when naming the notes in a Triad.

Here it is laid out differently

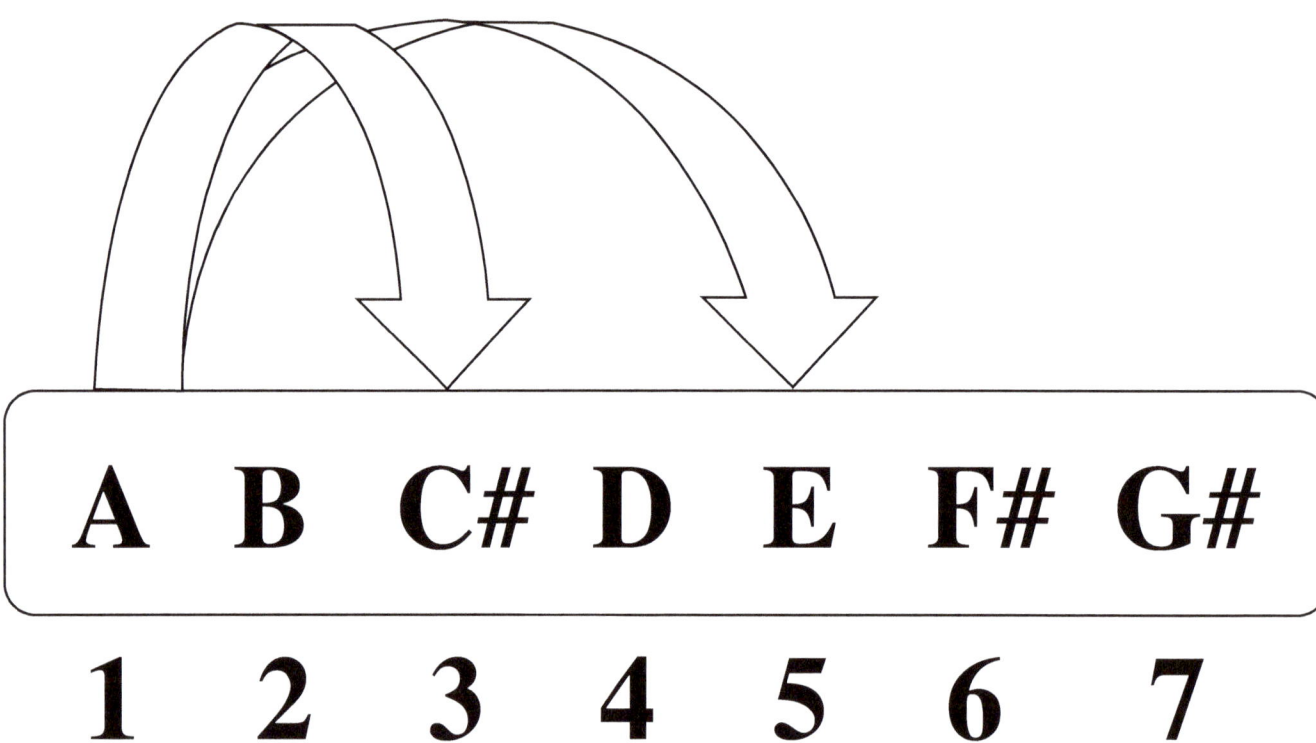

As you can see, the **A** is the 1, the **C#** is the 3 and the **E** is the 5. If you replace the C# with the Db, you are no longer using the 3rd, rather, you are now using a 4th.

Triads are ALWAYS 1, [some type of 3rd: Major or Minor] and a 5. While the notes **C#** and **Db** sounds the same, you must always refer to the 3rd note from the 1. In this example, the C# is the 3rd note from A.

Congratulations! You did it.

As a Coach for over 30 years, I realize what it is like to be a Coach as well as a beginner guitar player. This book combines the simplicity of teaching a beginner as well as a tool to help music educators teach their students.

Using Visualization

When learning (or teaching) something new I often tell my students to visualize. When learning an instrument, visualization tells your brain where your fingers will be placed. If you can't visualize it, your brain cannot direct you to place your fingers in the proper position. Give visualization a try when you are struggling with learning something new. This is not just for music lessons, but for life in general.

Practice Makes Progress

Let's face it, no one is perfect. The term "practice makes perfect" should be changed to "practice makes progress". And while this term is associated with a music lesson, it can be applied to anything we set our minds to.

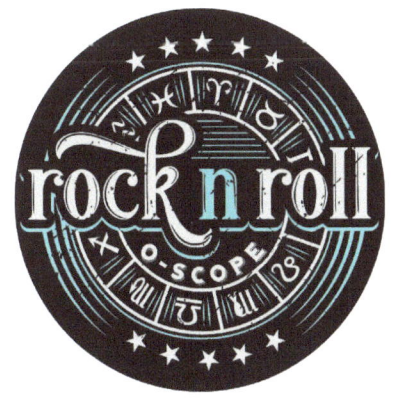

Revisiting Your Goals

We started this book with writing out your (or your students) goals. Now is a good time to look back at the 3 goals written down. Have you fulfilled your goals or are you still working on them? Regardless, it is important to set goals, whether it's for learning a new song, joining a band or landing your dream job. Goals can be anything your mind dreams up.

We love feedback!

If you have any feedback (good, bad or indifferent) please share it with us as we are always looking to improve the music lesson experience.
You can email me at michael@rockoutloud.com.

www.ingramcontent.com/pod-product-compliance
Lightning Source LLC
Chambersburg PA
CBHW060840290526
45792CB00006BB/2002